Poems from the Woods

copyright 2020 Byron Hoot

hootnhowlpoetry.com

Poems From the Wood came about, still come about, during hunting season. Which begins, for me, mid-September through nearly the end of January.

I hunt. I make no apologies for hunting. Nor am I interested in the arguments for or against hunting. Life is short, hunting seasons are limited. I am hunter. And a writer of poetry.

My father never hunted. Grandfather, uncle, cousins, an aunt's boyfriend and their stories told at Thanksgiving and Christmas entered into me and spoke and I said, "Here am I."

My father, though no hunter, was a preacher and that may be a type of hunting which knows no season and part of the reasons, just like the hunting stories, I became a hunter. A reader of sign. Someone who came to realize that tracks and sign and knowledge don't always lead to the destination you thought you were going to.

These poems have been written in tree stands, on the ground. Have caught me with pen in hand rather than a bow or rifle as a deer walked by as I considered just why I was where I was doing what I was doing.

"Hunting," I would remind myself finding the right word putting the notebook and pen away and looking and listening to the woods.

Of course I think the woods are the first sanctuary. These poems an offering. And hope that when you read them, they speak to you.

I have only followed the sign to bring you and I together here.

Namaste.

— Byron

Poems From the Woods

Table of Contents

Childhood	5
Fair Value	6
Falling Incense	7
Math	9
Calling	11
Avoidance	12
Seeing	13
The Measure	14
Betrayal	15
Investment	17
Taken In	18
Eyes	20
Hunters	21
Not Blinded	22
Tree Talk	23
Kinfolk	25
Readiness	26
Here	27
A Silent Look	28
Necessarily Two	30
Twilight	31
Teasing	32
No Words	33
Shadow Casting	34
Ready or Not	35
Declension	36
Among	38
Distance	40
Away	41
Not Prepared	43
Holding To	44

As It Is	45
You Come, Too	47
Beacon	48
Not Forgettable	49
Echo's Promise	50
Truthfully True	51
Dream	52
Just Now	54
Nuthatch	55
Midwifery	57
The Nature of Sign	58
Resurrection	59
Blending	61
Right Time	63
Remembering	64
Take Into Me	65
Tomorrow	66
Do	68
Time, please	69
Memory	71
Mist	73
A Little More	75
Beyond Capture	76
Not Sudden	78
Heard	80
That Step	81

Childhood

"Wheat or white?"

"White," I say choosing

The bread of my childhood.

So many things of my

Childhood I would choose

Today

    If I could.

Fair Value
I spent $41.00

Yesterday for three

Bags of groceries:

I am living in

The wrong place.

Falling Incense
There are certain types

Of rain I hunt in.

It waters down my scent,

Muffles my step,

Lifts the incense of damp

Ground up and around me

As if I'm in a place

Of prayer;

    Of course, I am.

How hard it is not to

Feel part deer and

Tree, sky and wind,

That force in and through

Everything in the house

Of the Lord not the one

We build, but the one

Where sanctuary is everywhere.

I hunt when the rain

Is incense falling

Down the way it is

This morning.

Math
I am not very good

At emotional math:

I carry too much,

Subtract too little,

The constant variable

Is always me and that

Makes the simplest

Equations unsteady.

I think there's an

Alchemist inside with

Algorithms and a set

Of scales and a ledger book

With two columns:

Enough,

    Not enough

        And he whispers

The answer in my heart

And then I know what

To say – Enough or

More, please

               And my

Heart balances again.

Calling
I call deer;

They don't come.

Same response

I get from God;

Still, I don't

Stop calling.

Avoidance

The great terror

Of hell is

Realizing you

Have lived in

Fear to avoid

What isn't there.

Seeing

The autumnal splendor

Of color is different in

The woods; there, sharp

And crisp is replaced by

Muted and blurred

Like the way Monet saw

The world where the familiar

Blurred, blended unclear

But still known.

                        Inside the woods,

The world of autumnal

Colors isn't quite like that –

Things aren't always

As they seem.

The Measure
At the end of the day when

It is time to leave

The woods, I look at

The light never time

Because minutes don't

Mean anything when light

Is the measure of all

Things.

Betrayal
The chipmunk running

Across the leaves may be

The echo of a deer who moved

The chipmunk out of where it

Was,

    Or the way ferns

Move in the wind their deer-tailed

Shape and autumnal yellow leaves

Magically hind quartered and legged,

Uprooted one royal, slow step

After another being made ordering

Everything within its presence,

Or the random, slow turn

Of the head to reveal the

Quietly stepping deer almost

Completely camouflaged against

The trees and ground it would

Have been unseen had the

Head not, just then, not

Turned around . . . the woods

Betraying the deer to be seen.

Investment

I have seen a dozen deposits

Of gold beech, red maple,

Rust oak falling

In the air made by some

Strong wind that did not

Touch the leaves on the ground

Only those in the highest

Parts of the trees –

The interest, the wind promised,

Will come up in spring.

Taken In

I have seen a tree fall

On a still day there at

Its base break away

From the ground and loudly

Lay itself down and then

Silence; likewise branches

Falling down just when they do.

I am not talking about the

Damage of storms, I am

Talking about when that moment

Arrives that can bear no

More and the heart lies

Splintered upon some living

Floor where love and life

And dreams continue on

As before and as often waiting

For the soul to take the heart

In and make it whole again

Like the slashings I see growing

Underneath the larger trees.

Eyes

I look for the horizontal

Among the vertical world

Of trees, that coat which

Absorbs the light rather

Than reflects it, that twitch

Which is not the push and

Release of the wind to spot

A deer moving.

                It is only

Among that which is often

Seen that that which is

Rarely seen can catch the eye,

The heart.

Hunters
My father hunted God;

I hunt deer... they're not

Too far apart.

Not Blinded
To see well

Always means

Getting the sun

Out of your

         Eyes.

Tree Talk

I am almost certain trees

Speak.

      They need the wind

To be Aaron to their Moses

Speech,

      But that is almost

Constant.

      Of course, strong winds

And storms are another thing,

But the daily speech of trees

Is heard easily.

          I don't know

What is said, but it is

So melodious, harmonious

I don't need to know a single

Word.

      Listen. That's all. Go

Into the woods and listen;

The trees are talking all the time –

Poetry, I think, it seems to me.

Kinfolk

I have seen a shimmering bush

Give birth to a full grown

Deer, seen a tree the size of my

Thigh cover a deer as though

A blanket had been dropped

Over it.

    I have seen the weary walk

Of hunters at the end of the day

Coming up trails walked on before

Land was sold and bought, before there

Were any seasons,

    When hunting

Was life and death and everything

In-between and heard the land

And trees and the deer call to me,

"Brother" and know where I belong.

Readiness
The unexpected is

What mostly

           Occurs.

Here

How do you describe stillness

With words?

You have to make the moveable

Unmovable,

What flows

Static,

What pulses

No beat . . . .

How do you describe

The holy stillness of woods,

An acorn here,

An acorn there falling

Eternities apart

And simply here?

A Silent Look

I watch the sun move

Upon the leaves as the wind

Breezes a shimmy

Through them.

Sunlight is not as solid

As you think moving,

Caught on trunk and branch

And leaf

      Which then cast

Shadows from their catch

Of sun.

      Which begs the question

Of the nature of light

And how steadfast, how

Penetrating it is.

Just pay attention;

You'll see what you've never

Seen before by looking

Into silence.

Necessarily Two

A sound without

A rhythm is no step.

There is a rhythm to the

Things that matter:

The ear hears

The heart's moans

Its lover's sigh.

Sound is just sound until

There is some rhythm

That matters.

Twilight
Above the trees the sky is light;

Beneath the leaves shadows.

Before long both will coincide

In night and darkness.

Teasing

The woods are doing it to me

Again: having me see what

Isn't there in the stirring

Of a leaf, rain unclinging from

Leaves, a falling twig,

A ricocheting acorn and I suddenly

Focus as if a deer has appeared.

It's an old game we play;

Sometimes, though, it becomes real.

No Words

The trees only speak

When the wind blows

That ancient guttural

Language slowly rising

Deeply intoned though

Sometime almost cracking.

I don't know what

Is said; they don't seem

To mind being overheard.

It's as if the sound carries

All the meaning needed,

The duration and rhythm

Never given twice the same way:

It gives great comfort

To me to be among

The speech of trees where

No words are ever needed.

Shadow Casting

The shadows of small birds

Increase their presence.

I have never seen a shadow

Correspond to the object

Shadowed – it's always

Larger.

    A matter often

Overlooked in the realm

Of shadow – the sources

Not as large they

Pretend to be.

Ready or Not

You can prepare

For anything,

But just you be

Ready when what

Occurs

        Occurs.

Declension

There are only two sounds

In the woods:

        Those coming down,

        Those coming up.

This I understand

And the fact there is no

Middle ground from which

Any sound is heard

Reassures me . . . there is

A simplicity here not beyond

Me. It takes a while to learn

This: squirrel, chipmunk, deer,

Turkey, bear;

        Then branches and leaves

And acorns, beechnuts, rain,

Snow – just because the last two

Are light does not mean they have

No weight when they strike, they do.

But I have found those sources

Of sound true within me:

Some come from the ground,

Some from the sky –

I listen accordingly.

Among
It sounds like rain,

But nothing hits my face

And when the wind stops

I realize the leaves have dried

Enough to sound like raindrops

In the wind.

                Now, a deer like

Me, will be betrayed by

Footsteps in the leaves

And by the nakedness of the tree

Nearly all the trees are bare.

It is no big jump to believe

How what can hide equally

Will reveal.

                It's just beyond

First light, one deer has already

Scented me and turned away:

Here, today, there is equality

As I hunt on the ground . . .

My two senses to the deer's

Three and the wind and

The sound of rain among the leaves.

Distance

The distance and my desire

Let my imagination shape

The body of a deer a hundred

Plus yards away from a blow

Down and branches that

Cannot be animated to life.

I think about distances

And imagination,

How what is close can be so infused

That what is seen comes alive

And what is far, too far way

Never moves and I have to say,

"No, not likely."

Away
The bar was noisy from conversation

That drowned out the music but not

The way the bar felt as if some favorite

Country song had filled everyone with that

Longing everyone knows about.

Camouflaged jackets and hats,

Marlboro soft packs on the bar,

Women, whose hands looked like a man's,

A certain equality and diffidence that fit

Right together.

    The three of us irregular

Visitors; the large draft $2.50 – it wasn't happy

Hour.

    At least not for the drinks though I wasn't

Blind to the faces, almost all, that held lines of stories

Sad, unspoken, unfinished,

But it was Friday night;

We were up from the city to hunt . . .

We came in between the drinks and laughter.

Not Prepared
Those oak leaves!

What jokers!

The slightest breeze

Moves them around

And they sound like

A deer walking through:

It's an above not a near

To the ground sound. . . .

Still, from time to time

I look around –

                In hunting

The moment you think

You know something is the moment

You're unprepared for.

Holding To

The cold that held

The snow now warmed

Lets it go melting off

Leaves and trees and ferns

And rocks.

      There is something

Here I should know

That crosses that imaginary

Line between Nature

And me.

      I don't think

I want to let that line

Leave quite yet –

There are some things I

Am holding I do

Not want to let go.

As It Is
What is the nature of the presence

Of God?

      We say it's love, but

We're cowards for saying so.

How is rain falls on the just

And the unjust? The wicked

Prosper? God a wind arbitrarily

Touching here, there, somewhere. . . ?

It is the fullness of God's presence

That changes everything:

Imagine being completely,

Unequivocally present

To someone you love, to something

 You do. What would a word like love possibly

Mean when you are fully present

And your presence changes

Everything not as you want

But as they want to be?

No wonder when God is present

The sinner and the saint eat

At the same feast,

You and I babble and

Understand one another completely.

You Come, Too
There are the sounds

Of pre-dawn,

Then first light, then

Light.

      I was going to tell

What I hear,

But I think it would

Best if you rose

Early and listened

For yourself.

Beacon
I left a light

On in the house I

Had not intended to:

I wish that

Happened more often.

Not Forgettable
Sometimes when I am

In the woods I have heard

And felt the heartbeat

Of the earth

            Loud and strong

Though not long.

It is not mine; mine has never

Sounded that loud, felt that strong.

Yes, reduced it would be

Exactly like mine, but it's not

Reduced.

      It sounds to let

Me know there is something

Between us I am not to forget.

Echo's Promise

Now is the time of year

Of the solo song of a

Single leaf falling.

Earlier, any breeze could

Create a symphony.

Now, it is the single leaf

Waiting for the right breeze

To fall in song in deep

Satisfaction and longing

And some intimation it will

Be heard again.

Truthfully True
I am always looking

For those things true

That hold a truth –

Not an easy

Thing to do.

Dream

Dream seeks two to make

Dream true.

    We do not dream

But enter dream and when

We do we are always seeking

Another.

    At least, I believe,

If memory – that great

Seducer of facts and lover

Of imagination – lets me

Recall this close to being so.

Dreams want two to become

One where eyes are stared

Into, where lips meet,

Where touch goes to the heart

And the self is absolved

And the self is seen as it

Has never been before

The language complimentary:

Two utterances, one statement

And yet the two do not lose

What has drawn them together.

Just Now
In a moment of eternity

The crow's caw

Against the falling snow

Is hardly out of place:

Those black, cacophonous

Notes against the white

Silent snow filling time and space.

Nuthatch

When I consider what is

And is not possible I

Recall the nuthatch

Who, as I hunted deer,

Was less than five feet

From me on the trunk

Then the limb of the white pine

And back again

          And then flew away.

I heard the hum of its wings,

Saw how quickly the head

Turned,

      Could not imagine

Those wings holding that

Body in flight. . .

          When

I consider what is and is not

Possible to do I see

The nuthatch in from of me.

Midwifery

Fantasy not

Imaginations

Is the Devil's mid-wife.

The Nature of Sign
The sign said, "Deer

Everywhere" but the

Deer did not appear –

Sign, I remind

Myself, is one thing

And what it gives is another.

Resurrection
Some leaf shadow shakes

On a blow down, the higher

Breeze missing the solitary

Leaf like some old man's

Hand weakened by use

And dying nerves.

                This is

What I do not understand:

That leaf, in time, will green

Again and again endlessly:

Is there not some life I

Give from my death?

How do the just desserts

Of heaven and hell

Compare to the resurrection

Of a leaf? How is that?

The crowning creature of creation

Once here forever gone.

Some frost or snow or wind

Will blow that leaf down

Off its limb,

                And then it

Will come again.

Blending

The sound of cars, an occasional

Plane, are all around me.

I am listening for the footfall

Of a deer misplaced to draw

My eyes. There is this

Dual reality in which I live:

My IPhone is in my pocket;

A bone handle knife at my waist.

I cannot completely chose

One over the other and must

Trust my sense of two

Worlds is wrong in the most

Fundamental way . . . my clothes

Synthetic blends,

My eyes and ears and the deer

And the woods as they've always been.

Right Time

I check my watch

For time but not

For the timing

Of things.

    The difference

As deep and wide

As an ocean

Though timing subsumes

Times.

    Time cannot place

What is anywhere.

Beware: Just because

It's time doesn't mean

The time is right.

Remembering
When I don't see

A person often

I tend to forget

Or miscall their name;

Of course, this doesn't

Happen with God.

Take Into Me
I like the way

When I'm hunting

Deer suddenly appear

And startle me out

Of my attention to

The awareness of their

Presence as I breathe

Slow, try not to move,

See if the moment will

Hold a shot or not.

Of course, I likewise startle

Them into my presence:

When I am seen

They flee. . .

            There's much

About a deer I would take

Into me.

Tomorrow
I am too tired to walk

And not interested in climbing

A tree stand so I set here

Among some rocks and a tree

Overlooking a slopped ravine

Of twenty or thirty feet.

I know deer cross here.

I have taken deer

Here before but I don't

Know what choice they

Make that meanders them

This way.

    But I am here

At the end of day,

Last light, snow too long

Held on branches falling,

Looking. . . .

        I think

How much deer and I

Are alike and so won't tarry,

Walk out in last light,

Come back tomorrow.

Do

After you have done

All the right things,

All the wrong things,

Then you can finally

Do something.

Time, please
Why is it we put the hour

Before the minutes

When asked what time it is?

How secondary

We treat the minutes

Of which the hour is made

As if the whole, the hour,

Is greater than its parts,

The minutes.

                It doesn't

Seem right to me.

We do the same thing

With eternity pretending

It is something other

Than now.

           When time

Is so disfigured no

Wonder we can't figure out

What time it is.

Memory
                  The relationship

Between memory's accuracy

And its reliability tenders

A conclusion that may let

Both be what they are without

Condemning either for not

Pretending to be otherwise.

We rely so much on memory

And yet so often the details

Of a memory are not factual

Though perhaps accurate for what

Is remembered.
                  How can this be?

The accuracy of memory

Lies in the recreation

Of the feeling not t he fact

Remembered exactly,

Not the details clear as a bell

Ringing

        But in recreating what

Was felt: from these feelings

All memories flow

And the words to make them so.

Mist

The damp, mist-filled

Quietness draws what

Sunlight will refuse.

Fog is sister to the moon,

Brother to the night

And to be in a morning fog

In the woods raises

Questions answers do not

Satisfy, creates scenes

And feelings unsought,

Turns the way

A knife trims meat off

The bone of a deer.

The staccato rhythm of rain

Caught then pushed off trees

By the wind – one, two;

One, two, three; one two three;

One, two, one – draws

Something deep inside

Towards this fog burning

Off in sunlight unstoppable

Light that will not be denied.

A Little More
In a moment the fog thinned.

Not slowly, not suddenly

But in some form of immediately

What was unseen became

Clear and the fog disappeared

With the faintest dust of its mist

Languishing in the air

                        And what

Could be seen and what could

Be heard was more than it had been.

Beyond Capture
I cannot say how light

Works in the woods,

How it shows,

Then hides in its moving

Slant of eternity what

Needs just that moment

To be seen and then

Goes covering, uncovering

A hillside, a swale, a valley,

A stream

      Or what the presence

Of deer and squirrel,

Turkeys, nuthatches means

The way the eyes look

To see.

      I would be amiss

If I denied how the ears

Are affected by the eye

And how this is a reciprocity.

None of this can be captured

By words; even a picture

Cannot contain what the eye sees.

Not Sudden
How slants this day towards night

The skull cap of sky uneven

At every horizon and the colors

Strewn, woven by some madman

Shuttling a tapestry with God's

Burning kiss of desire incensing his

Heart in prodigal design seamlessly

Making the imperfections the perfections

Of the living. . . ? This mixing

Of day into night is no miracle

Of a magnificent trick demanding

A slight-of-hand, a distraction

To create what would not

Naturally come.

                    Nothing like that

This slow honing away

Of day to night's razor sharp

Edge of darkness that cuts

Through everything.

    The darkness

May be immediate but it

Will not be sudden – nothing

Ever is.

Temptation

It is the time of day

When eye and ear say, "Stay

Here! Stay here!"

    And there

Is nothing seen nor heard.

They do this a lot,

Seduced so easily by the desires

Of my heart.

Heard

How do you know

What to hear

When you're listening?

Hearing everything

You'll know what

You're listening for.

That Step

Small the stride,

Certain the step

That gets you to

The top and bottom

Of a mountain.

Made in the USA
Middletown, DE
10 December 2021